Beach Boy

NEIL J. FOX

Independently published.

ISBN: 9798707174087

First Printing, 2021

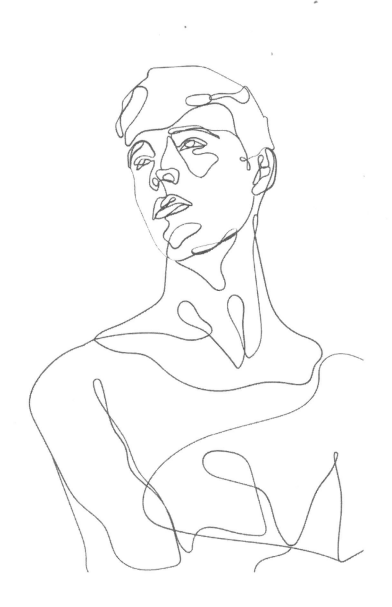

This book is dedicated to those who dare to dream – to the people who do not want to be defined, or judge others by one given thing. This is for those who strive to do more, be more, and see more in others, and ourselves.

CONTENTS

"The real voyage of discovery consists not in seeking new lands but in seeing with new eyes."

— *Marcel Proust*

The Sun

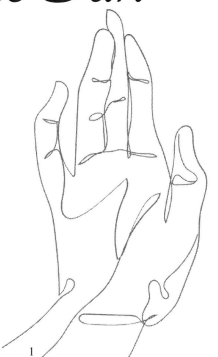

JACK OF ALL TRADES

It's time for you to meet the Jack of All Trades
Who could play the Queen of Hearts, and even the King of Spades

A man who can fit to whichever mould he needs
Whatever is required of him, constantly aiming to please

The hats he wears differ in size, matter and style
Each holding its own responsibilities, expectations and trial

Someone you can rely on to get the job done
Remaining content, as long as he still gets to see the sun

The thing about the boy is he can be anyone you want him to be
The greatest of actors, not yet trained academically

Each to their own, people hold their perceptions of Jack
His awareness of these differing narratives, often difficult to knack

Everyone believes to know him, this well-grounded guy
But do they know…

That all he has ever wanted to do is fly

WELCOME TO THE BEACH CLUB

Welcome to the beach club
The finest in all the land
This exclusive destination fabricated from sea and sand
A manifestation of this world at hand

Welcome to the beach club
Where the proletariat and aristocrats cross paths
A place that through the summer the wealth resides
And the less well-off more often than not thrown to the side

Welcome to the beach club
Where the lines in the sand are clearly blurred
Of those who are relatively happy, and those who are sad
The poor unseemly sane, and the rich are even more mad

Welcome to the beach club
A destination that contains no truth or certainty
Conversations held here are conceited and figural
And sex on the beach is something even more literal

Welcome to the beach club
Where those who are undeserving are clearly not welcome
An unrightfully prejudice, exclusive and elitist place
Existence of which in this day and age, our fall from grace

Welcome to the beach club
Here, perception is the highest valued currency
The lines of perspective never meet, skewed with despair
As we're reminded once more, that nothing in life is truly ever fair

HANDING OVER MY HEART

A permanent commitment
Resistance to my own choices
Second guessing myself some more
Another step towards self-declared victory
Creaks loudening on the hard-wood floor
And finally - everyone's going to know the score

In my hands my beating heart
Atmospheric hypertension
I'm used to tending to the beat of my own drum
Heavy pounding and tougher thumps
Sensitive, and even slippery some
A nerve-wrecking transplant analogised to none

My darkest fears forming a clot
The weight of my world in my trembling hands
Releasing it free from my grip with a sigh of relief
No longer held captive under my chest
Torn from my limbs as the ink drips with grief
From life's tree, sprouted this beautiful leaf

In the act of this vulnerable exchange
The blood begins to splatter across the floor
Seeping through the cracks, suddenly considered ceaseless art
My existence becoming everlastingly immortal
Losing control was always going to be the hardest part
In this operation, of handing over my heart

SUN BUM

Every day
I seek the warmth of the sun
I am selfish
Often driven by this desire
And equally at times gluttonous some
My longing for the light sometimes overbearing
Sacrificing other opportunities
Which become a loss
These built-up bricks become walls
Holding out any other opportunity cost
Because I am blinded by the light
Laser-focused and losing sight
On the glorious radiance of summer's daylight
It's not a bad thing to find what you love
A reason to keep going
To make it through the dark nights,
And the at times, even darker day
As I strive to beam in the sun all day
But behind the science of every sundial
Is the significance of scale
The equilibrium of our priorities
And every now and again
The importance of a little hail

THE HIGH ROAD
(HAIKU)

Often hard to reach
The high road's summit is
Heavenly sublime

I AM AN ISLAND

I am an island
And that is okay
I have grown and become sheltered
In some and every which way
I don't consider myself remote
But more simply just astray
From the mainland's ever-expanding bay
Don't let me be misunderstood
I will always welcome each element
As well as the sea, the waves,
The wind, the stars, the sand
It is not exclusive or elitist
I'll stress to say
I am simply just an island
Flowing with the way the wind blows
Operating on my own accord
Here is home to indigenous thoughts
I enjoy the peace this way of life brings
The promised land promised
Is a stone's throw in the ocean
An island in the sea, out past the bay
And from the mainland's touch
Slowly, I move further,
and further away

RUBBING SHOULDERS

I'm getting closer to the life I want
Rubbing shoulders with the other kind
I sit, I watch, I observe
Try to understand their movements and actions
How they got to where they are
A place in life that often seems *oh so* sublime.

Through the valley,
I still have so much further left to go
Taking any direction where I can
Following the signs that I have come across
And in my own interpretation of them
They don't always come across all that clear at all.

The people that I meet along my journey
I try to take from them what I can get
Sourcing the information that I can
Listening, and learning contently and calm
Sometimes, only just watching from afar
Absorbing the tips and tricks that I can take and run.

Cause if I'm rubbing shoulders with the right kind
I want to make sure I remain resourceful and smart
Taking full advantage of the surroundings I've been presented with
Grateful for these close encounters to explore the others' mind
Figuring out the path to get there myself, on my own grind.

A DOLLAR

What would you do for a dollar?
Would you let a baby cry?
Would you deprive somebody of an opportunity,
and never tell them why?
Would you take another's life?
Would you commit atrocity or crime?
Would you wipe yourself of your dignity,
lose all your respect and simply sigh?
Would you sell your soul to the devil?
Would you give away your time?
What are you willing to sacrifice in your life,
in order just to get by?
Would you partake in treason?
Would you get involved with fraud?
What are the lengths we are willing to take,
or even willing to try?
What would you do for a dollar?
I want to know understand what we are capable of
Yet I truly don't mean to pry,
I just want to know if we would still be able
When all is said and done,
to look ourselves in the eye.

SANDCASTLE

All I want is a home, with a view of the sea
I've even had a look
A place where we can be happy
Cause I've peeped the ending of this book

So, you go scoop some water for the moat
I'll stay here and mind the land
Working together endlessly
On this castle made of sand

And I hope to the heavens it'll stand tall
Through all the wind that's sure to come
Our home out here among the dunes
To the shore we will have swum

This House of Kings may as well be made of bricks
These walls are solid as a rock
Cause we're the foundation of this château de sable
Impossible to knock

LONG DAYS IN THE SUN

Too much of a good thing
Sometimes seems like never enough
Until it can be too late to see
The evening chill coming breezing in
And the regrets of overindulgence sets in

The realisation introduced to us only by hindsight
As the skies, clouds and stars gather
The elements join forces
Eventually pushing away the sun
And only then,
We can finally see the damage done.

The Moon

9 LIVES

Every now and then I think of the struggles
we've had, and how we thought the world would eat us up
and I continue to look back, eternally and remorsefully glad

The people I dearly miss, the one's I've passionately kissed
lovers that are now considered strangers, to me,
and this new life that I am living since they once existed within it

Gathered groups of pals collected, that were ultimately
cast aside, not all by choice or permanently, I insist to add
with rogue time travelers appearing once again in modern times

The weighing pressures we've previously succumb to, and falling
victim to what we thought would hold us back, heightened ideas
and
exaggerated outcomes we feared would arrive, never coming to
pass

Worries we never felt we'd be free from, held captive of our own
biggest fears, fearing for the future, and what was inevitably to
come
as if we held no control in what could yet, and still can, be done

Every role we ever embraced has been a building block of who we
were, are, and becoming, each one we wondered, whether it would
stick, and survive, and outlast the other eight

These contradicting and contrasting versions of me, defined
traits contain multitudes and differ from mind to mind, seen as this
person I once was, to those who only knew me then and there

In the mix of our lives, this current version of who I am, is just
as fluid as those before, not knowing if this my final form,
deep down knowing a greater evolution will most definitely derive

You could say that I am carrying, that I am possibly with child,
brewing the next version of me, the latest upgrade of my psyche
at full-term, waiting to birth another of my many cherished lives

SOMEONE'S CHILD

Do you know that girl you work to shame
The one who's name you fail to frame?
A woman for whom you'd simply die
To secretly lie beside
Do you know she's someone's child?

The quiet guy minding his own time
Keeping to himself, out of harm's way
Who can't ever pass your presence without
Some wise input for you to say
Do you care he's someone's child?

What about the people who mean no harm?
Ones you'll never come or care to understand
Going about their life, their own kind of style
Called to court forcefully to face your trial
Do you mind they're someone's child?

Should we work to care as less as those people
And drown out the urge to pursue a person's motive
Trying to understand the actions of an inflated ego.
I wonder, if pride is held so high while we roam the wild
And if you remember, you too, are someone's child.

MANTICORE

There is much to be said about the company in which we keep
Those whose time we spend like currency
In exchange for ideas, with opinions reaped
Walking into the bar they steadily arrive
Leaving more than an impression, this impressionable five

The fire breathing dragon is the first in the door
Contributions to conversations more often heated
This great winged creature,
With wildfire we were normally greeted.
And as time went on, things stayed much the same
My own breath beginning to spark its very own flame

A werewolf claws his way through the entryway
Marking his territory through the darkened door
Friendly but still, growling at times.
Occasionally letting out an aggressive roar
Spontaneous reactions let out in spur
With each howl heard, I felt my limbs start to grow fur

I grew concerned when my forehead began to sprout a horn
Growing several feet long as time went on and on
Eagerly listening to these stories told.
Brought to us, from the perspective of this great unicorn
Galloping through myths and magical tales,
Our minds captivated, sworn free from scorn

To the left, there was the most beautiful mermaid laying around,
On the ground, of which she made a glistening pool
Dripping water as each tale was told
Audiences forming pulling up the next stool
Her stories enchanting as long as her tale,
As time went on, my skin began to scale

It wasn't long until I felt my owns limbs change
From my body I once knew, I became estranged
Unbeknownst to myself I was now somebody new
As the centaur spoke, he joked of his specific woes
Surrounded by all kinds of beasts,
This new creature rose

So, what was left of little old me?
The naive audience member listening free
Taking it all in even more than I thought
A transformation over time, I never needed nor sought
Out the door, I was a man no more
Instead, my very own breed of a manticore

AT WASHINGTON SQUARE PARK

One last trip around the block
Finishing our final victory lap inside the park
The course was blind-siding
And the finishing line untimely stark
The end is inevitable, and we both know
It's goodbye to the warmth of the summer sun,
and hello to bitter winter snow

We shall let our tears dry another day
And think of the times that have since past
All the moments spent side by side
Together alone, we are, at last.
Through the highs and lows of the race
We finally found our privacy
At the close, in this very public place

The birds gather around our feet
Picking away at what is left of our crumbs
Our supercut now soundtracked
By the sounds of the NYU students and their drums
And right here, laid out on the grass, we shall lay
Our memory forever etched into the nearby bench
Among the trees, the leaves, the litter and the bark

Here then, now and forever,
At Washington Square Park.

SAME PAGE OF A DIFFERENT BOOK

You have your say
And I have mine
And we will continue to dance
This magnetically charged tangle
And let it untwine.
You dip, I catch
I flip, you twirl
Our energies displayed
Across the stage floor.
Passion, the only choreography
We happen to know by heart
Frolicking through deafening silence
To the sound of our own songs
To the rhythm of our finely tuned tunes
It is made very clear to recognise
Just like the man of science and the man of faith
If anyone was to simply take a look
That those two are on the same page
of a different book

ALIEN BEHAVIOUR
(HAIKU)

In the eyes of small minds
Is going against the grain
So other worldly?

TWO WHITE PAINT PATCHES ON THE ROOF

Clear signs of a story untold
Symbols
Of life that was once lived
Here, but back then
The tale of which they would tell
Two little white paint patches on the roof
Igniting my imagination
Here, and now
The possibilities unravel through the night
How did they come to be?
What chapter of their love story that those were born
Perhaps, maybe it was even something more dull
Like that of a burst pipe
But I simply do not care.
Because I am hopeful
Here, and hopefully later
That those who will come after us
May look up and see our those of our own
Two little white paint patches on the roof
And wonder
Curious if love was a part of this story untold
If it had any part in their creation
And they will, and it did

THE PRIDE PARADE
Dedicated to the victims of the Pulse Nightclub Shooting June 16ᵗʰ 2016

Finger on the pulse
On the trigger of change
Edging ever so close to glory
Dodging our demise by an inch each time.
Please tell my mom I love her
If it ever comes to it,
If I don't get one last chance
If she never gets to watch me have my very first dance.

Because not so long ago we had no voice
No right to speak, no space to talk
Don't ask, don't tell!
And now here we are, still having to walk
In this rebellion for rights and respect
Storming into the sun, and out of the shade
We will fight back year after year to come, and even then some
At the pride parade

GHOST TOWN

I walk the streets of this once familiar town
Only, it's winter now
With every step forward, I seem to move back in time
Back to a period of my life when you were to have worn
The crown
But the queen of this castle has well and truly resigned
Now this distant derelict kingdom
Is nothing, but a ghost town.
The paths are lifeless and pale
With a chilling air sending shockwaves through my spine
Every now and then, I think of how our lives could have been
What could have happened
What we should have never seen.
I can't help but wonder as I walk these streets
Would the leaves of these trees surrounding me still be green,
Livelier than they are now
Than this deathly brown
If you were still to wear the crown.
But that was a time in my life which was led by a lie
I was never fit to rule the kingdom I was offered
That part of me has died
Overcome, reflective, yet content with the outcome,
I am a different person roaming through
this unfamiliar ghost town
And in the sorrows for my old self,
Still, I cannot help but drown.

ROOM 10

Here we are again
Where reality feels imaginary
Here, in the midst of room 10
Peggy Lee serenades of black coffee
As we take a fitting sip to the soaring sounds
Heard within the 5 o clock shadows
Of the dimly lit grounds
Stepping through time, in search of the pool and cottages
The early morning moonlight guiding our way
In what is rightfully now, our playground
Roaming the castle walls, we have succumbed to
Infatuated in the idea of those who have come before us
Walking the walk, hand in hand
We are creating our own history
As they once were.
The history that reeks the halls
The faded carpets littered with tales of folklore
In this transcendent place,
The castle on the hill still stands true against time
Where the damaged reputations of stars lie,
Many of which here, have come to die
In the darkened corners, where secret romances thrive
Thinking of how lucky that we have come to be
And of those who stumbled across these same carpets
Creating their own movies, in which they had starred
Falling deeper and deeper in love
As we now are.

The Sea

FOOTPRINTS IN THE SAND

I want to prove
That I was here
That I made an impact
And had something to say
Something to live for
And something worth dying for
That my time was truly spent
Every penny of my energy
Exchanged
On memories, achievements and
Accolades
That I learnt to better myself
Leaving a small mark
On a big world
Made valuable change
That I made those around me
Feel something
Whether a snigger or a laugh
I want to prove
That I was here
That I left footprints
In the sand
And not to waste this
Incredible opportunity
That I have been gifted
Called life
So many people don't live
To their full potential
But that is their choice to make
I want to make sure
That when I am dead
And gone
My legacy
Will live on and long
Whether I am
Considered
A genius
A jack of all trades

Or
A master of one
Or maybe even none
I am
Indifferently idyllic
As long as I know
I tried
To live the best life
I could
That I walked every corner
Of this land
And that when I was told to sit
I would stand
That I gave to many
A helping hand
But most importantly
I left
Footprints
in the sand

COLOURS

I am yellow and I am blue
I am every shade and every hue
Navy, baby, electric, and even royal too
I am every crashing wave colliding,
Every shade of the vastly deep sea
Can't you see?
I am every individual grain of sand,
From the darkest orange to the lightest yellow
I am each moment of the sunset spilling over the land
I am every time of day that the sun is bright
Yet, I am the darkest corner of the blackest night
Could that even be right?
I am as deep green as the densest forest,
Lighter tones of a lime as mellow
As emerald as the nation's meadow
Because I am yellow and I am blue
I am every shade and every hue
We are more than what we are painted to be
There are more colours beneath that of which the eye can see
Look closer

MELTING POT

Cold concrete walls
Warm in some places
But only for a few fleeting seconds
Where they had just been touched
Moulding like melted candle
Wax drips.
My eyes beaming red
Faded lasers trying to pierce
The squared walls
Moving towards the floor
Weakening in strength
Sourced internally from the core
The heat of my body burning
Misshapen and not yet finished
Melting
Fanning the flames and converting my vessel
To something unknown
The lasso is tightening
Closing in
And gone
Something even stronger
Cooking
Ready to be reborn

MAKING WAVES
(HAIKU)

Ready to rock the boat
Making waves when needed most
Be the change we need

ATLANTIS ADJACENT

Right when I least expect - it happens
As the last few drops of my coffee pour, right after I've collected
the post from the foot of the door
I find myself lost in the lost city, built on the foundations of the
opportunity cost
Spent, by previous choices I, myself have made

I roam free through the streets made up in my mind
Wandering through the kingdom that never came
Yearning for a life that does not exist
I grieve, because maybe, I just may not have let it

In the rare moments I am now alone
I am accompanied by the greener grass on the other side
And for just a moment, I lay in it and cry
Contemplating the alternative route, I should have taken through
life deep down inside

And as I grab the post, and take a sip of my coffee
I allow myself to wander for just a moment in time
To an alternative universe that had potential to survive
And I remind myself, that everything is fine

For the rest of my days, I will live Atlantis adjacent
Reflecting on the life beyond the fence that stretches outside my
window
Because nothing will ever be truly good enough
But I can't afford to be too complacent

LOST AT SEA

Winds of solid rock, at gale
Blustering seas, anchored
Kept down by hail

Submerged, steering south
The surface sprints further north
For success exists a ravishing drouth

Remaining breaths numbered
Three, two... I count
Refusing to fail, I fight the slumber

Losing sight of what lies above
My vision grows shrouded
Aquatics overhead act as flying doves

Suffocating on the inhaled pressure
Being swallowed alive in the midst
Finding hints of pleasure from the hidden treasure

Seeking growth within the challenge
From the depths of the darkest seas,
I scavenge

Do not sound the sirens when I am lost at sea
I need not be saved nor rescued
I am where I have to be

MEETING A MERMAID

When I was just a kid,
I always knew that mermaids exist
Even in my adolescence, I was sure
Beneath the surface society had created
They were kept at bay
Far away, from what was deemed as normal
Afraid, if given the chance,
At what they might say

Regardless, I remained adamant
I was certain
These creatures could exist
I knew that they were real
Living within an underworld
Beyond the fairytales we were told
On this planet which we shared
This unapologetic creature roamed

You see,
I wanted to swim like a mermaid
To tackle the currents with confidence,
With a passion and a flair
Live the life that I was supposed to live
Immersing myself in a new world unknown
One I didn't know where, but I knew
I belong

And when the moment finally came,
Once upon a time,
To discover that mermaids actually exist
I managed to hold it together, I insist.
I simply watched from afar in awe
From the coast, I watched them effortlessly swim
Confirming my suspicions,
Slowly, dipping my own toe in.

Knowing, that they were real
Is all that it truly took
To get me into the water waist-high
Alas, it didn't come to me over night.
There were skills that I had to learn and train
Which came to me over time
Because to strengthen my new backbone
I had to break a rotting spine

And now, I swim like a mermaid
I tackle the currents with confidence
With a passion and a flair
I am now unafraid of the unknown
Day by day, I assess the seas in which I swim
Gauging, if I'll feel unwelcome and ignored
Or be something that is celebrated and adored

RIVER

The seeds I've sowed have sown
The fields I've tended to are grown
Sunflowers singing towards the sun
The wildflowers are matured, and it feels
As though my work here is truly done
And now,
After all is said and done
They shall whither
And at that point I know
I will call out for you
My River
To flourish the world that I have known
To stream down from the mountains
I have won
And take me away with you
Overboard and overcome
Washing away the world that I have known
Bringing me to new destinations
I could never have found alone
Pool by pool, they form a river
To flourish a new and greater land
A level playing field with greater crops to fuel
More seeds to sow, and work to do
My River
I will call out for you
Take me away
River won't you run to me
Oh River,
Won't you come to me

CHANGE

The world is changing
And so are we
A place demanding
Of more inclusivity
Still, I wonder
Why people are so enraged
At the simple idea of
Change
That is keeping our world clean
Repairing the damage done
For the future
Of our earth and sea
For our next of kin
Those we know
And them
We may never get to see
A world
Where including others
Is occurring
With welcoming arms
And if I may say,
Just because
You don't understand it
Just because you cannot see it
Hear it
Breathe it
Experience it
Does not mean
It is not
Real
Or valid
Our culture is based
On relatability

What makes us
Laugh
Cheer
And cry
But when it is not
Relatable
Those issues
Are pushed to the side
My simple ask
Is please
Do not resist.
Accept
Embrace
And love
Change.
For a home
Where everyone
Feels welcome
Accepted and safe
In themselves
And the planet
And a society
That we can
Look on
In our graves
With relief
And think
Our kids
Will be
Okay.

BEACH BOY

As darkness folded, and the light awakened
He arose that dawn
Another day of adventure to spend
Under the world's eye
Subject to interpretation of others, at odds with his own will

He past the sundial atop the clocktower
Casting it's ever-moving shadow, in constant shift
Finding residence, he lay atop the sand
Overlooking the earth's edge
On the front line facing out towards the unknown

Many onlooker's past, going about their day
On their own journeys along the coastline
of chatter, gossip, silence and even retrospective thought
With a quick and passing glance, their opinions cast
In a fleeting moment, none were dignified, yet all held true

To some, to all, to one, to none,
He was as mellow as the sand was still
With the same potential aggression of the crashing waves across
the coastline
Considered waste, like the washed-up bottles on the shore
And as weak as the lacking heat from the sun's unimpressive beam

Indifferent to the silent judgements emitted
Going about his day as originally planned
Subject to opinion, he lay in his subjectiveness
Because from the sun to the moon, the sea to the stars,
From dusk to dawn, his day was irreversibly idyllic

He understood the fluidity of one's perspective
Never fixed, like the shadow of the ever-moving sundial.
That the world we live in was painted,
With the blurred lines of water lilies
And the magic we have been granted to alter our own mindsets

51

Because to the scarce, the few, but more importantly himself,
He was as calm as the sand was still
As determined as the waves crashing across the coastline
Hopeful, like the washed-up message that lay hidden within the
bottle, if one had cared to notice
And as bright as the blinding light that came from the sun's ever-
impressive beam

Because no matter how far as the eye can see
Is never quite enough to see the detail that lies on the other side
As vast as the multitude of moods felt in a single day
Beauty lies in the eye of the beholder's perception
Fear residing within the eyes of the narrow-minded

With that, he found warmth in the hug of a chilling sea-breeze
Seeks comfort swimming above the depths of the darkest seas
Kindness in the actions of judgmental strangers
The duality of man is questioned, if not multiplied
As we stand, on the fine line of perspective and perception

Where the water meets the land
He is the waves, the ocean, the wind,
He is every grain of sand that collectively creates the coast
He is the sun, the heat and the light, the first sign of the shore's
twilight
He is each and every component that makes up the beach

The captain of his own soul
He vowed to constantly broaden his horizons
Seeking answers in other's intent, then solely in their actions, to try
to understand
And as the shadow of the sundial dwindled at dusk
He slowly began to sink into the sand

The Stars

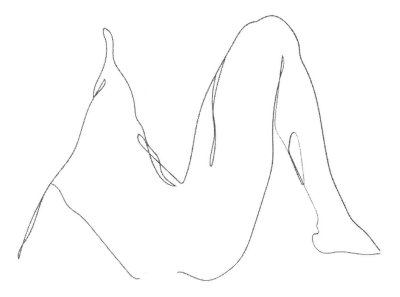

IMPRISONED WALL FLOWERS

The vines fall tangled towards the ground,
slowly stringing along
Pouring over the painted pot from their roots
a beautiful song
Their melodies strung,
they harmonise together to a halting bridge
Quilting the gaps that could simply just be left
a song unsung
With no intentions
to cause such alluring havoc and disarray
These imprisoned wall flowers
can have so much more than expected to say

TROPHY

Hang me on your highest wall
Polish me like solid gold
Hold me to your highest regard
Your greatest glory never sold

Tell them of your admiration
Of your greatest achievement to date
A suited home with pride of place
It was neither destiny nor fate

Place me on your mantel
At the top of the crowded shelf
Shine a godly light upon me
That you wouldn't even believe yourself

Imprison me in a bell jar
For safety, to help ease the mind
Never let my colour fade
Letting my powerful glimmer go blind

Because I want to be your greatest feat
I just want to make you proud
Look towards the future with delight
A burst of gold to battle away the clouds

COWABUNGA, BABY!

The 4th of July
The land of the free is sparkling
Written in fire across the sky
A nation blazing from the Atlantic
To Malibu and back
Taking orders and swerving corners
Supervising sodas and salted snacks
Sneaking shots in even creakier cabanas
Fleeing from the grip of the prison guards
Not yet loose after 2 to 3 bottled beers
And yet I am front and centre still
I've got the best seat in the house
Watching the movie from inside the silver screen
Cowabunga baby!
The reflections of multicoloured lights
Surfing the black waves
Although fixed to my assigned position
Intuitive timing and assumptions of limited intelligence
Makes for somewhat exquisite escapes
Sharing flashes of over-glorified glee
Joint efforts to catch ourselves during a mutual flee
Even then, as much as I hate to admit,
I couldn't feel more free

BEYOND THE BOARDROOM

There is a life that exists
Beyond the boardroom
Where you don't get sucked in and swept up
That is plentiful, fruitful and rich
To leave work at work is a promising deal
For a life that is real, with limited risk
Because beyond the boardroom
Is a world of complete enrichment
A place to accomplish your dreams
Where you prioritise your own fulfilment
And your soul blazingly gleams

THE REBEL ROLE MODEL

Struck like a lightning bolt
Oddly fitting like a glove
Cannot be defeated or defined
Of admiration, we followed with love

A rebel with a cause
The unlikely selection by common jury
The reddest berry, cherry-picked of the bunch
Overflowing with benevolent fury

A contagious connection tough to construe
To the status quo, a leader of anarchy
Expanding mindful horizons
Through unbeatable and unwavering energy

An inspiration that just feels right
Striding the path less followed in a confident fashion
Through this rebel role model, we regularly gain
These outpouring waves of pure and potent passion

YOUNG HOLLYWOOD

Shots of sake off of Hollywood and Highland
The lights of the city below, glittering like diamonds
I've killed the reality I once knew to be true
Living in a dream that I had once dreamt
Drinks filled with liquors we've never heard of
With strangers who aren't our friends
Nothing lasts forever
Except for tonight in my mind
We cheers to the dreamland
We've made of our lives
Tell the driver to take the long way
Through Mulholland for the view
Play that song that we once knew
That sang of a life like this
It went something along the lines of do-do-da-do
I've finally put myself first
I came as I am
And tomorrow I'm leaving a better man
Hungover and a little dehydrated
I am happy.
How many people can truly say that for themselves?
I've found the entrance to the secret garden
And the gate is somewhere between Sunset and Santa Monica
Nestled between the bosom of boujee hotels and strip clubs
High up in the hills,
We pour another drink and cheers to nothing
We are privileged, but we are grateful
Hoping tomorrow will never come
We get messily graceful
And for tonight,
We are young Hollywood

MTV RAISED ME

I grew up an infant, in front of the box
Eager eyes, watching on
Pool parties of empty pools
With people performing their catchy rock songs
And then it evolved.
I became engrossed in the house's that they held
Plaques and trophies proudly displayed upon the walls
Lines of cars appropriately placed
I didn't want to settle for anything less
I wanna do it all, I would think to myself.
I became obsessed
Not with a life of over excess
But with the idea that anything is possible
That if I can put my mind to it
I can make my own dreams come true
I can be like them. Me.
I can be the M in MTV.
I held zero interest in being from a small country
And an even smaller town.
I believed in a bigger world that was made for me
That was full of endless possibilities,
And that I, myself, was credible
Of all potential capabilities.

NORTH STAR

(HAIKU)

The North Star calls out
My next adventure awaits
Beyond the window

SUNDOWN

As golden hour begins to rust
The sky finally folding in on us
We'll lay on the grass to let our eyes adjust
And with twilight's chill creeping in my bones
Now as our day is coming to a close

I'll be with you at sundown

Shortly we'll watch the daylight turn to dark
The silhouette of the city's shadow stark
Reflecting on the day that's done
The endless laughs, the priceless fun
For now, and forever I'll hold you close
At each and every sundown

And when sundown finally strikes
Alone on the grass
My knees held tightly in my arms
Looking out upon the fading view
Questioning the way the world works
I'll think of you

I AM GOD

Of my ideas
I created a world
Of love and loss
Hope and despair
Hurdling it up into the air
Still, it sat amongst the stars
A moon
Lighting the night
And from afar it looked small
Insignificant
And like anything else
Passable
But if you looked closer
You would really see
Something bigger
Of perpetuity.
Beaming
Existing
And real
A manifestation
The fruit of my labour
Ripe and ready
For digestion
Observed and examined
Each idea
A bluebottle
Buzzing around
My cluttered mind
Opening the window
Clearing the noise
Setting them free
A representation
Purely
Of me

The Dusk

QUARANTINE
(MARCH 2020)

Fantasias playing on the television
The colours the most vibrant I've seen all day
The violins from 1940 still thrillingly played
Probably a level louder than they should be
The sims deluxe is downloading
As the paints on our self-portraits dry
The sadness and fear in my face
Is at war
With the golden glimmer of hope
I'm secretly hiding inside
These days don't feel much like living
As we live through this moment of
World history
Letting some of my planned life goals go
Trying to take back control of what we can
Stimulating our senses with past pastimes
New consoles and even some games
Older than ourselves
Tomorrow, *Future Nostalgia* is released
And I couldn't find a title more fitting
For this time in which we are living
The umpteenth Groundhog Day
Holding my breath that it stays this way
In a sense
My only goal to make it out alive
With those who I entered with,
Making it safely out the other side

MORNING'S CALL
(HAIKU)

It's sad to ponder
The beauty of morning's call
Is not seen by all

KUMBAYA

Beyond the hilltop meadow,
sat a man, sitting alone by his campfire
The other side of the hill
'Kumbaya', he sang along
By his lonesome, he was going strong
'Come by here', he called out in a desperation so dire
In search of still waters,
He was a man trying to take control of fire

Quietly chanting Kumbaya, he yearned
By the third verse of his fourteenth attempt,
He was eventually joined by another,
Who strolled into his inner circle with supreme serenity
Silently, they took a seat beside the man
In the company of, the embodiment of peace he now was.
Whom of which he kindly asked for their advice
In learning how to take control of his fire

All this time,
He was able to sustain a manageable campfire,
keeping the flames alight yet tame
A game of backgammon, back and forth they fought
Beside him they spoke, a confident speech so eloquently soft.
In which they said;
'Keep singing your song
Don't sing for others, but only for an audience of yourself
Don't seek the validation of others, of which you cannot keep
It cannot be bottled,
like the fire in which you reap.
Instead, let the voices speak
Contradictions in life are essential to exist
For every judgement made, we are to obtain five ourselves
We must understand the complexity of human nature
And that in itself, can be hard to do
But to take control of fire,
You are capable to fan the flames of which you speak

You must learn to live your life as only you wish
Not the life decided for you, by the company
You may or may not keep'

The man was startled,
but not because he had learnt something new
But because he had been told something
of which he always knew to be true.
And so he sat beyond the hilltop meadow,
Alone by his campfire
With still waters in sight,
A man who was learning to take control of fire

SUGAR-COATED KISS

You call me handsome
I call you unsure
Settling it like adults
You tell me
'You're very mature'

As we kiss goodbye
Back to our own separate lives
'We'll be in touch'
We say to each other
We both know deep down
Never to end up seeing one another

So, we put it to bed
And we kiss this goodnight
It was short while it lasted
Nevertheless, an utter delight
Leaving the scene of the unsolved crime
With nothing but unresolved doubt in my mind

You and your antics I'll miss no doubt
As we decide to part ways
With a sugar-coated kiss
'I'm sad', I desperately confess
One last kiss
None the less

COWBOYS AND INFLUENCERS

The old wild west for a new age
The internet it's battlefield,
As they go to war
All trying to outdo the other more

The world we knew has changed
One step forward, two steps back
It's a given that history will repeat itself
With everyone only in it for themselves

Nowadays, the cowboys and influencers are rife
In a fight to the death, for followers and likes
We try to distinguish the difference between the two
This newfound culture, hoping to bid adieu

Because they're trying to coax us
Into living a dream of a reality, that just isn't true
Fooling us into buying the next big thing
We must free ourselves from the lasso of this rodeo ring

The Old Wild West for a new age
The internet it's battlefield,
As they go to war
How much longer do we have to watch this for?

27 CLUB

Sitting in eternal isolation
Gives you time to reflect
On the 27 years past
And the ones I hope to have left
Reaching this stage of life
Is a reward in itself.
The accomplishments I've made
Sit pride of place on the shelf
As I come up to the dreaded crossroads
Between what is considered young and old
Having to make life or death decisions
On whether to check or fold
I welcome the change with open arms
As I approach the entrance to the 27 club
Plucking the next of my roses
From life's nettle-filled shrub

I STILL MISS THE DAYS WHEN IT RAINS IN LA

I still miss the days when it rains in LA
Driving through the city and I'm singing in the rain,
This place loved for the sun, a permanent holiday,
Here I am in the mi(d)st, feeling this type of way,
the rain comes crashing down a storm
When it rains here, it pours, and I finally
Understand the validity of that statement now
Can I keep you, to the sky I ask aloud
Do you want to keep me too?
Pedestrians laugh as we pass
Men and their dogs,
Iced coffees in hand
We'll meet on the corner of Hollywood and Vine every time,
pick me up from the bus station
Holding me in your arms each time
Through the canyons, we'll cruise
All the way down Ventura just like the old days?
Losing myself in the music of the city,
I walk with a soundtrack to my steps
not able to see the wood from the palm.
We broke up but I still feel like there's a chance,
because I still miss the days even when it rains in LA,
it makes me feel like I belong,
because nothing is always perfect,   '
every moment of any day.
How the streets would turn to sunken streams
And highway rivers run through the city strong
Let me meet your demands,
I don't want much or to use you for what you have,
I just want you.
It wasn't supposed to always be this way,
but here I am,
and I still miss the days when it rains in LA,
Because you're just a dream some of us had
But with all the hopes and dreams
and the promises we made

Down the drain they all got washed away,
the sins we had, you and I, LA
I'll keep them close, in the hopes
That we meet again someday
Until then, I'll reminisce on the days it rained
Because it was in those moments, I knew
My companionship to you was forever claimed

MY DEAR FRIEND

My dear friend
Comes to me at the most unexpected times
On the darkest of nights, I hear the door knocking
A breaking and entry of kinds

Although not always welcome, he confidently arrives
To disturb the night which I had planned
Making himself more than at home
Bringing with him, melancholic memories at hand

I am somewhat guilty in enjoying his presence
Letting him have his say
Allowing him to swallow the atmosphere of the room
His presence is notable, and here to stay

In the midst of the melodrama
He reminds me of the times past
How much life has changed, and what could have been
From reality now, a stark contrast

Despite the despair he has brought
I allow myself in the moment to wallow - just for today
Eventually, he will come to go, and I know for sure,
Tomorrow will be a better day

DAISY

Strolling through the meadow
We were often led astray
But then you gave me a daisy
And together we made a chain
With every day that followed
Feeling like an endless summer
We were dancing in the rain

FINDING MY FOREVER HOME

When my body and soul have finally come to end their courtship,
and I am on the lookout for my forever home

Allow me to set up camp along the Isle of Doagh
Watching over my homeland from its most northerly point
How noble
Where I will watch the ones, I've come to know
And those I've come to love and cherish
Live on and long
Within a respectfully peaceful distance I will remain
In tow

It goes without saying that a piece of me will always be present
Either in person or in spirit
Or even perhaps
In a perfectly polished ornament
In the north facing room sitting above the double-sized windowsill
That rarely saw nothing but shadows constantly in search for the
sun
Somewhere where time was well spent dreaming of a land
Where I would call my forever home

If I had to pick between a local hidden pier or a popular
promenade
My response would be, "maybe both"
A reflection of how my life was lived
Never wanting to settle on any one given thing
Always striving for more
For every cycle on the unwinding country roads down to the pier
To bask in a few moments of hidden heaven were filled with joy
As those spent walking, running and swimming alongside the
infamous Blackrock

But how could I possibly not find a home along Franklin Avenue
The silver lining where the lived-in streets and the land of endless
possibilities met
Where tears were a relief, and the laugher was so hard it was sore
Where luck was imminent, and I grabbed every opportunity with
full steam vigor
Squeezing every last little piece of chance that I could grasp
Before my time was inevitable to come to a close
Residing in this place where I felt more freedom than I ever
possibly could have known

And when my body and soul have finally come to end their
courtship, and I am on the lookout for my forever home

Cast me like a net along the Atlantic Ocean
So I can capture within it the secrets of the world which lies
beneath
The ocean becoming my final form of divine being
Because if you can't beat 'em, join 'em,
And I intend to.
Skimming the seas from coast to coast, where so much of my
heritage lies
I will finally allow the power of the sea to succumb me
Allowing me to finally face the fears I once frantically dread

Or perhaps, perch me within the gardens of Fernhill,
High up in the Dublin mountains
The tranquil bliss in this place where we had the chance to reside
Together, it was here we found our harmonious place to hide
Each evening as the leaves of the trees danced across the carpet,
shortly after six,
A place so peaceful, we couldn't hear the turbulence of the traffic
passing by
Scatter me among the leaves and I will dance forever as my final
oath
Overlooking the south side of the city, and all along the way to
Howth

And when my body and soul have finally come to end their courtship, I will have found the many habitats in which I shall call home…

Particularly a strong contender along the Pacific Coast Highway
Where the Santa Monica mountains meet
The stretched shorelines of the beach
Not having to make a choice of which of those I prefer, as people there tend to tirelessly ask
But settling on a resting place that simply encompasses all of the above where I may bask
So, lay me to rest smack bang right in the middle of Malibu
Because whether you are to decide which is more relevant; imaginary or true
This is where I have been living my whole life
The entire time with you

The Dawn

YOUR WORLD, MY WORLD

I occupied my days in scenes of blue
In search of skies, similar too
Often filled with melancholic moments
That was the old me, but you

Swam through life in a sea of red
Rose-tinted glasses, with opposite intent
A burning building of flaming frustrations
No signs of fanning out, and then

Lanes merged, a sudden crash
Forming a new and unexpected lilac path
We were found, skipping through purple rain
Living in lavish lavender, just like that

Nothing was ever the same
Previous problems overcame, no one to blame
Your world became a thrilling track which took wings
Your song now sung over silver strings, and I

Found something greater than expected
I became an awarded miner, of life's great expedition
Mine to own, a prize to behold until I am old
My world became gilded, in solid gold

WAKING UP ON CLOUD 9

That morning has come around as promised, once again
Delayed moments my eyes spend
to fully awaken from the blinding strain
But this time I have awoken,
Far away from where I used to consider home
Somewhere in Dreamland,
I could have only ever imagined to have known

Testing the strength of my senses, I explore
and examine every little detail
Trying to understand my current surroundings a bit more
Within this celestial abode,
I feel further and further away from the ground
The morning alarm breaks the silence
Startling me as the trumpets sound

In the ways of an eager historian, I am curious
Eager to explore my most recent subject
Secretly, hoping for a result not spurious
I search for clues to understand
Brow raised, and suspicious to find
Anything that I can hold onto
With my findings safely enshrined

What did I ever do to end up here?
What have I done to deserve this hand of cards?
Is heaven as heavenly as this moment appears?
The alarm repeats once more
Reminiscent of a Main Street Disneyland parade
It brings me back to reality
My happiness from this particular morning yet to fade

A breakfast follows, fit for two kings
Tasting menus to satisfy all curiosity
The dawn of the morning springs
We sling ourselves across the comforter
Back-to-back daytime TV on a roll
We sink further into the clouds
I grab another bowl

I take a break to walk atop the clouds
Taking in the magnificent views
Here above the noise and the crowds
Admiring the fallen houses upon the hill
Perched in their place of residence, they're stuck
I see my reflection in their windows
Elevated, and can't believe my luck

Because I wake up here, and you're there
Looking you in your eyes
You run your fingers through my hair
Tossing and turning until noon
Morning's like this are what makes life's taste so divine
There's a certain richness to the flavour
Waking up on cloud nine

MY LIFE AS AN ACTOR

Life can be sweet
In Paradise Cove
This world that I've created
And this story that I've told

This tale is one for the ages
These parts that I've been playing
In this, my greatest role yet
Not much preparation for it do we get

As I awake every morning
Like a seasoned professional, I learn my lines
Preparing for this acting role
Not many can read between the lines

This land of make believe
Where we are all playing a part
A role to be filled, an actor billed
Standing ovation for a performance off the charts

The job requirements are never ending
I've played many roles in my day
A child, a student, a mentor, a teacher
Versatile talent, if I so may say

'Fake it 'til you make it'
You have heard those before, you preach
At times I want to leave this dead-end job
Head stage left, and right to the blissful beach

HALL OF MIRRORS

Take a walk through the hall of mirrors
And tell me what you see
Objects in the reflection may be distorted upon view

A long, lonely stride for any straggler
Walking further from reality, once inside
Many an adventurer have withdrew

Presented with yourself in many forms
People who pass must find their inner strength
Their character, on the firing line for review

The hall of mirrors holds a kaleidoscope of colour
Often an opportunity to see yourself in new light
Here, you see every shade, and every hue

The reflections of yourself can be at-times unsightly
Misshapen, with a twisted representation
More likely misaligned, from what you thought you knew

In the hall of mirrors, there is no single reflection
That is accurately and wholeheartedly true, however
All of it is you

MONKEY SEE, MONKEY DO

There's nothing more powerful
Than to show them how it's done
Swinging tree to tree,
The outcome is second to none
Gripping the vines tight
Is just one part of all the fun
Diving in the deep end
And swimming towards the sun
So lead by example,
And continue to make leaps
While jumping through the jungle
Proving the possibilities of landing atop mountain steeps
Fear not, and don't fret if they don't immediately follow
Just make sure to stay consistent with your run
And as time goes by,
Eventually, they may very well may come.

TRAIN OF THOUGHT
(HAIKU)

On the tracks of life
The train of thought never stops
But can be controlled

COMMON GROUND

When you created a glass ceiling,
I started to build myself a stair of solid stone
To rise above and carry on,
Stepping on every misconstrued underestimation,
Each acting as a powerful steppingstone.

Alas, let us find common ground
Atop the glass ceiling that I have now shattered
From your failed attempts of stopping me in my tracks.
I shall not be pigeonholed or have my capabilities capped
Free to achieve what I believe I can.

Here, I stand in a line with those alike,
Forming a chain of an unbreakable bond
Together, we sing in a choir
In perfect harmony upon our newly crowned stage
We continue to rise, we levitate, we fly.

There are no grounds for prejudice, or unjust hate
Still, we welcome you to join us if you will,
And you should -
This place of serenity is nothing like anything else around,
And the potential here, is truly renowned.

AFTER LIFE

For a moment,
I had it all figured out
I thought I knew what I wanted in life.
Meeting with friends at weekends,
We would discuss the plans we had all pre-planned
Blueprints, to our seemingly short-lived lives
Focusing on what we wanted the most
And for me, it was simple...
Fancy clothes and shinier shoes
Manors surrounded with perpetual land
A growing reputation of power to mount
The steadily expanding income of an even healthier bank account.
An aspirational bunch, sharing our shared objectives over brunch,
We would discuss in detail what we sought out of this life.

It wasn't until later that evening, when a storm finally came
Lightning struck, and it hit a nerve
No longer seeing the light, in what I believed to be right
I realised that I never considered what I sought - in the *afterlife*.
I struggled to ponder,
What would be my lasting impression?
What was my contribution to the world?
How will I be remembered when I'm gone?
These were all questions, I failed to comprehend
So, I thought.
And when the storm had finally came and went,
Something significant happened to me that night
Because it was in that moment, I decided
that I would write.

CHARACTER

Who are you?
Have you made a conscious decision deep down inside?
To objectify our individual character goals
At one stage or several, I believe that we have all tried

We must understand if character is really chosen
If it is something for us to truly decide
Whether we as people browse a catalogue
Picking a suited personality to live out with pride

In reality, it is with every brick we form,
Cemented together, the perfect storm
Stitched piece by piece through the act of living
Is when true character is actually born.

Because in our very own stories, we are the lead
It is in every other book in which we feature
We must be conscious of how our character is interpreted
As a knight in shining armour, or a great-winged evil creature

When it comes to the perspective of other protagonists
In the library of storybooks, we play many a role
Nothing to fear but simple misunderstandings
Knowing who we really are, deep down in our souls

It is the content of our character
We have the power to control each day
Alas, on how it is understood
We are not the ones, who have the final say

The ease of accepting misconceptions is more often rare
It is one of life's hardest lessons to learn not to care
The collision of opinion on our character
Will always hold a constant home up in the air

So, who are you?
Is it really ever for us to actually decide?
When it comes to how others will tell tales of us
With perspectives, the only power we have is to guide.

LIBERTY AT LAST

Heavy are the chains I've held in my fists
Dragging along by my weakened wrists
Weighted down by ton weight of thought
Shackled to the ground
By the depths of public perception

Looking on in admiration of those who run free
Whipped by chains at every bend
Tackled by sour scourges of judgement
Poisoned by preconceived notions of character
Continue on their journey through the straight and narrow

Yet, here I am, held captive and trapped
In this pigeon-hole mindset presented by others
A great misunderstanding of our minds potential
And as we grow older,
I feel the prison grow smaller and smaller

As some seek comfort in the darkened box,
I see a crack of light, a shimmer of hope
Illuminating the small space, I have found myself succumb to.
The key: my freedom of expression and thought
Freedom to challenge what we have been presented with
Freedom to even just try –
Freedom to learn, change, expand and fly

And now the golden ray has begun
To burn away slowly, at this shield of grey
Distracted by each and everything that I can finally see
Thoughts of summer flings that the sunshine brings
And the smells of sprouting daffodils and daisies
Slowly, begin to bring me back to life

Here, the waterfalls are flowing north
Trying to find a cloud to crash against, in place of rocks
Yet – there is no stopping them.
My perspective has shifted,
I am lifted
Now I am elevated and towering towards the sky.

This feeling may not last forever,
No fixed destination fit for a full circle finale
As in this game of life, it will likely come to pass
But for right now, I am free
And I can truly feel
Liberty
　　　　at
　　　　　　　　last.

Chateau Marmont

HOLLYWOOD

Thank you, once again, for supporting my second book. I hope you find some freedom in the poetry. The main message I wanted to convey is that the perception of others doesn't matter, as long as you know who you are and that you are capable of anything.

Nothing in life is black & white and we are all monticaros in our own way.

Many, from Room 10 —

Neil JF.

8221 SUNSET BOULEVARD HOLLYWOOD CALIFORNIA 90046
TELEPHONE (323) 656-1010   FACSIMILE (323) 655-5311

BEACH BOY

The dawn of the Beach Boy has arisen. The second book by author Neil J. Fox, Beach Boy, is a collection of poetry that centers in on the topic of character, breaking down not only the fundamentals of who we are, but who we are perceived to be. Along with the ideology that we as humans are multi-dimensional beings, many of the poems narrowly finds the balance between the fine line of perception and perspective and the importance of awareness and acceptance, all while asking some hard-hitting and thought-provoking questions along the way. It's time to enter the world of the Beach Boy. Will you too find liberty at last?

As a collection of poetry, Beach Boy covers many topics including love, loss, self-actualisation, perception, contradiction and the multi-dimensional nature of humans and our character. In the world of the Beach Boy, nothing is black and white. Much like life, people are multi-dimensional beings, often constraint to stereotypes or categories, as a means to try to understand us easier. We are more than just what we are classed as. We are unique. Society tends to categorise, classify and stereotype people into one category in an attempt to assume an understanding into a person's actions and beliefs. In Beach Boy, many of the poems explore the multi-dimensional nature of our being, and how we are more than just one colour on a colour wheel, we are the whole wheel.

ABOUT THE AUTHOR

Neil J. Fox is an author that has been featured on the Amazon UK Poetry Best Seller chart with his debut poetry collection Dreamland, Somewhere Else in 2019. A native of the West of Ireland, he has always been involved and interested in art and its many forms, coming from a creative family. Having emigrated to the United States twice, Neil has experienced what is widely considered "The American Dream", having resided in Los Angeles and New York.

Following the completion his master's degree and climbing the career ladder within the tech industry, Neil released his first collection of poetry, which details a journey of self-discovery and understanding one's identity by exploring themes of origins, life and death, and the trials and tribulations faced throughout the individual growth we each experience as we journey through life as the protagonist of our own story.

His highly anticipated second collection continues to explore themes of self-discovery and acceptance, finding the fine line between perception and perspective, as well as uncovering the multi-dimensional nature of our character. Along with writing the book, Neil is also responsible for all aspects of the book's creation from formatting, editing and designing his collections independently in its entirety.

Follow Neil on social media under the username @bruthaniall.

Printed in Poland
by Amazon Fulfillment
Poland Sp. z o.o., Wrocław
20 February 2021

aff9bf5b-a6c2-4e3f-8c99-1b8a5d765a4bR02